Fresco

By Henry Israeli

POETRY

New Messiahs (2002)

Fresco

SELECTED POETRY OF

Luljeta Lleshanaku

EDITED WITH AN AFTERWORD BY HENRY ISRAELI
INTRODUCTION BY PETER CONSTANTINE

Translated, with Henry Israeli and Joanna Goodman,
by Ukzenel Buçpapa, Noci Deda, Alban Kupi,
Albana Lleshanaku, Lluka Qafoku, Shpresa Qatipi,
Qazim Sheme, Daniel Weissbort, and the author

A NEW DIRECTIONS BOOK

The author, editor and translators would like to acknowledge the following journals in which many of the translated poems first appeared: *Chiron Review* ("Only the.Beginning," "On a Night Like This"); *Crowd* ("The Woman and the Giraffe," "The Woman and the Scissors"); *Fence* ("More Than a Retrospective," "Half-Cubism," "Out of Boredom") ; *Grand Street* ("Fresco," "Peninsula," "Once More About My Father"); *The Iowa Review* ("Memory," "Winter"); *Modern Poetry in Translation* ("Self-Defense," "Our Words Have Grown Old," "The Almshouse," "The Silence"); *Perihelion* ("Yearly Snow"); *Pool* ("Birds and Carbon," "Always a Premonition"); *Seneca Review* ("Electrolytes," "The Night Will Soon Be Over . . . ," "The Moon in November," "The Habitual"); *Quarterly West* ("Seasons Change," "Frail Bones"); *Tin House* ("Neurosis," "Betrayed"); *Visions-International* ("Quite by Accident," "What Is Known," "The Awakening of the Eremite").

"Electrolytes" also appeared in the *Anthology of Magazine Verse: Yearbook of American Poetry 1997*, edited by Alan F. Pater (Baker & Taylor, 1998). An earlier version of "Season's Change" appeared in *Visions-International*.

Design by Sylvia Frezzolini Severance
Manufactured in the United States of America
New Directions Book are printed on acid-free paper.
First published as New Directions Paperbook 941 in 2002
Published simultaneously in Canada by Peguin Books Canada Limited

Library of Congress Cataloging-in-Publication Data

Lleshanaku, Luljeta.
    [Poems. English. Selections]
    Fresco : selected poetry of Luljeta Lleshanaku / edited with an afterword by Henry Israeli; introduction by Peter Constantine; translated, with Henry Israeli and Joanna Goodman, by Ukzenel Buçpapa . . . [et al.].
       p. cm.
    Includes bibliographical references.
    ISBN: 0-8112-1511-3 (pbk. : alk paper)
    1. Lleshanaku, Luljeta—Translations into English. I. Israeli, Henry, 1967– . II Title
PG9621.L54 A25 2002
891'.9911—dc21   2001052140

New Directions Books are published for James Laughlin
by New Directions Publishing Corporation,
80 Eighth Avenue, New York, NY 10011

Contents

Acknowledgments

I would like to thank Joanna Goodman for sweating over some of the translations and helping to edit and arrange the rest, Caroline Crumpacker for her advice on ordering the poems, Peter Constantine for introducing the selection in more ways than one, and Peter Glassgold, Peggy Fox, Barbara Epler, Declan Spring, and all the staff of New Directions who made this book possible.

I would also like to extend my gratitude for the hard work and long hours contributed by all the Albanian translators; in particular Ukzenel Buçpapa and Shpresa Qatipi, who shouldered the brunt of the work. Without their invaluable participation this collection would not have been possible. I also owe Dr. Buçpapa very sincere thanks for first introducing me to the work of Luljeta Lleshanaku. I am indebted as well to Albana Lleshanaku for enduring many hours of questions regarding the particularities of interpreting translations from the Albanian.

H. I.

Luljeta Lleshanaku is a pioneer of Albanian poetry. She speaks with a completely original voice, her imagery and language always unexpected and innovative. Her poetry has little connection to poetic styles past or present in America, Europe, or the rest of the world. And, interestingly enough, it is not connected to anything in Albanian poetry either. We have in Lleshanaku a completely original poet.

The fact that she is writing in Albania today is significant. There has been an upsurge in Albanian literature following the collapse in 1990 of the harsh Stalinist dictatorship. Poets and novelists who had grown up in a totalitarian society that was in many ways more oppressive than the darkest years of Stalin's reign in the Soviet Union were given almost overnight the freedom to write. Established poets like Fatos Arapi wrote new and candid verse, while the younger poets were energetic but rudderless after having been nurtured on Socialist Realism. All this poetry that came out of the hope, fear, hunger, and despair of Albania's desperate post-Stalinist 1990s is wild and creative, reflecting the chaotic but hopeful situation in Albania. Albanian literary critics eyed this development with a mix of fear and ecstasy. Unruly though the new writing might at times have appeared, what was apparent was that it was very original, because the poets had had virtually no contacts with the literature of the outside world. Lleshanaku's voice is the clearest to come out of this melting pot.

The unusualness of contemporary Albanian writing is linked to the unusual course of Albanian literature, which has the curious distinction of having both a long and ancient tradition, but also being very new. At the turn of the twentieth century, Albanian was the last of the European languages without an official writing system. (Turkish was the official language.) Writers who chose to write in the spoken Albanian idiom used Arabic, Greek, or Latin script, depending on their education. The bulk of modern Albanian poetry was still oral and epic, sung by bards— "A living laboratory for the study of ancient times," according to Ismail Kadare, Albania's foremost writer. The dichotomy between an ancient oral and a new written literature stems from Albania's turbulent history. While the rest of Europe was experiencing the Renaissance and the Enlightenment, Albania was under Ottoman rule, which viewed the Albanian language as a dangerous nationalistic weapon and forbade it to be taught in schools or used in any official capacity. And while Europe was in the midst of the literary ferment of the early twentieth century, Albania was still trying to establish an alphabet and making the first attempts at a national literature. Gjergj Fishta, a national folk poet, finally proposed a standardized Latin orthography, which was adopted in 1909.

Luljeta Lleshanaku was born in 1968, during a crucial turning point in Albanian history. The People's Socialist Republic of Albania was celebrating the twenty-second anniversary of its Stalinist regime. Seven years earlier Albania's dictator, Enver Hoxha, had isolated himself from his last ally, the Soviet Union, outraged at Nikita Krushchev's denunciation of Stalin, and shifted his allegiance to China's Chairman Mao. When Mao launched his devastating Cultural Revolution in 1966, Enver Hoxha vied to outdo him. And he did. A great anti "-isms" campaign was launched in Albania to cleanse literature of all non-Marxist elements and "alien ideological manifestations." Poetry and prose were no longer to be tainted by: abstract humanism, anarchism, bourgeois objectivism, bureaucratism, conservatism, decadentism, ethnologism, folklorism, formalism, imperialism, individualism, intellectualism, mysticism, nihilism, patriarchalism, revisionism, or sentimentalism, to name a few. Many foreign books were banned, among them the Old Testament, the New Testament, the Koran, the Talmud, and all Buddhist texts. Albania was declared the first atheist nation of the world, and churches and mosques were torn down or converted into warehouses or local "culture" centers. Ancient icons and religious monuments were destroyed, precious books and manuscripts were burned. Poets and novelists were forced to volunteer to strengthen their ties to the land by working in the fields. A piece of writing that manifested the slightest deviation, or perceived deviation, from the new official policy could land a writer in prison, a labor camp, or worse. As many poets were to find out, even the most unequivocal Communist stance in a poem was subject to being interpreted as anti-Communist propaganda. Visar Zhiti, for instance, a twenty-two-year-old rising star on the Albanian literary scene of the early 1970s, was persecuted and finally imprisoned for ten years after sending his poetry manuscript to Naim Frashëri Publishers. The verse that triggered his downfall:

> No, no,
> No bootblack will ever shine my shoes!
> I do not want people at my feet.

To the untrained eye these lines might represent a youthful call for equality. The censor, however, interpreted them as an outright expression of capitalist-bourgeois contempt for the toiling bootblack.

And yet one of the unexpected results of the Albanian Cultural Revolution was that many prose writers turned to poetry, since it proved easier to follow the strict guidelines of Socialist Realism in the more concise forms of verse. While Lleshanaku was growing up, poetry was everywhere: in books, magazines, leaflets, on the radio. There were many public readings. The first poems she would have encountered would have followed Party dogma closely. Much of that poetry is difficult to read today with its rambling proclamations of party ideology. Some major Albanian poets of the 1960s and 1970s, such as Dritëro Agolli, managed to express their Communist conviction in strong language, without a trace of irony:

> I would have crawled through the mud,
> Crushed and pulverized, crippled forever,
> My arms slashed off at the elbow,
> Rather than utter, "Long Live King Zog!"
> But I sing Enver Hoxha's praises.

And in another poem Agolli writes:

> I carried the earth of your fields
> In a woolen sack
> Under my coat
> To bring it
> To the Writers' League.

Other poets, such as Ismail Kadare, chose themes that endeavored to steer clear of anything that might possibly be seen as ideologically questionable. As had been the case with writers during the darkest years of Stalinism in the Soviet Union, successful Albanian poets and novelists became master jugglers of nuance and evasiveness, which at times led to powerful works despite the impossible strictures. Much of Kadare's poetry (and prose) centered on the distant past, with Homeric or Ottoman themes:

> To me you were as impregnable as Troy,
> A Troy I could never conquer.

To me you were indecipherable,
More indecipherable than the Etruscan inscriptions.

Only in my dreams, ah, in my dreams
Have I grasped your thick hair.
I felt more delight in conquering you
Than all the Greeks felt at the fall of Troy.

Only in my dreams are you decipherable,
You, my sweet Etruscan girl.

In a country where reading was one of the only pleasures still allowed, the poets who managed to publish were guaranteed a wide readership, as miners, longshoremen, and factory workers lined up to buy their newest books. The People's Socialist Republic of Albania, with a population of three million, was a nation of poetry bestsellers.

Though Luljeta Lleshanaku was born at the height of Albania's Cultural Revolution, she was raised during the even darker years that followed. In 1972 Richard Nixon traveled to Beijing, and Enver Hoxha, outraged at what he saw as Chairman Mao's betrayal of Communism, began distancing himself from China. A decade and a half of Albania's total isolation from the outside world and increasing oppression followed. There was an almost complete moratorium on the circulation of foreign books, and translations of foreign literature practically ground to a halt. In his recent essay "The Dictator's Library," Bashkim Shehu, one of Albania's foremost young novelists, took a walk through what used to be the restricted "R" section of the National Library in Tirana—the only place in Albania (besides the Dictator's luxury villa) where one could find a French copy of Agatha Christie, Baudelaire, or the Dictator's favorite contemporary French poet, Edouard Glissant.

Aragon and Rafael Alberti had been accused of betraying Communism, like Sartre, who was even accused of being a key representative of French imperialism. I found many books by Sartre, even an Esperanto translation of *L'existentialisme est un humanisme*, and another on microfilm. Why have the National Library order an Esperanto translation of a book, and a microfilm, only to stamp a restrictive "R" on them? Also restricted was a bibliography of the works of Cervantes—which, I admit, was totally beyond my comprehension. And then came a whole series of R's covering the whole philosophy section, from Plato's works and Aristotle's *De memoria et reminiscentia*, all the way through to modern works, among them a Cuban edition of Hegel's *The Phenomenology of the Spirit*. Even the philosophy books of György Lukács, the staunchest Marxist critic of the twentieth century, were restricted. The whole of philosophy was saddled with R's, except for Marx, Engels, Lenin, and Stalin.

The major poets who had established themselves in the '50s and '60s tackled the new state of affairs in different ways. Dritëro Agolli, who became the president of the Albanian Writers Union in 1973, was perhaps the most successful poet of the 1970s. (His 1974 long narrative poem *Mother Albania* sold over a hundred thousand copies.) His work became increasingly ideological, though he was not above turning to his readers in a stage-aside:

> Forgive me for being a bore,
> For filling my poems with didactics,
> With workaday agitprop.

Mark Gurakuqi and Luan Qafëzezi, a generation older than Agolli (they were both born in 1922), wrote almost exclusively political poems that are practically unreadable outside the parameters of Stalinist Albania. Other poets, such as Dhori Qiriazi, published less but tried to balance propaganda with nonpolitical poems. Many other poets simply fell silent.

Luljeta Lleshanaku was seventeen when Enver Hoxha died in 1985. During the next five years the People's Socialist Republic of Albania, still a Stalinist state under its new dictator, Ramiz Alia, began to disintegrate. After over a decade of absolute isolation from the world, with most of its national budget poured into armaments, Albania had run itself into the ground.

The dictatorship finally came to an end in December 1990. The first years of liberty were perhaps even more frightening and chaotic, as Albania's infrastructure continued to crumble, one government after the other collapsing, but for the first time in the country's history there was complete freedom of expression.

Lleshanaku quickly established herself as a powerful poetic voice, but one totally contrary to that of her generation. Her contemporaries, who had come of age with the decline and collapse of the Stalinist state, wrote verse loudly voicing the terror that had been and the terror that was perhaps to come. There was a strong literary reaction against all the norms and precepts of Socialist Realism, and yet political and social themes continued to be the principal driving force behind most of Albanian poetry of the late 1980s and early 1990s. Poets who had been raised in a literary world of Socialist Realism were ready to react against it and attack it, but had difficulty breaking free from its schooling. To quote one of Albania's foremost poets, Koçe Petriti:

> My soles were ripped, I patched them up.
> I know what stone lies in my path.
> I tread on it and write on it
> my own humanitarian verse.

But one of the elements that distinguishes Luljeta Lleshanaku's poetry is the absence of direct social and political commentary. Her poetry's remarkable variety of themes, which avoids simplistic reactions to a terrible past and an unstable present and future, is perhaps one of the elements that makes her poems contemporary classics of world literature. The imagery and rhythms captured in the masterful translations gathered under these covers make her poems as compelling in English as they are in Albanian. She speaks individually to her readers, the mark of a true poet able to transcend time and culture.

PETER CONSTANTINE

I

MEMORY

There is no prophecy, only memory.
What happens tomorrow
has happened a thousand years ago
the same way, to the same end—
and does my ancient memory
say that your false memory
is the history of the featherhearted bird
transformed into a crow atop a marble mountain?
The same woman will be there
on the path to reincarnation
her cage of black hair
her generous and bitter heart
like an amphora full of serpents.

There is no prophecy, things happen
as they have before—
death finds you in the same bed
lonely and without sorrow, shadowless
as trees wet with night.

There is no destiny, only laws of biology;
fish splash in water
pine trees breathe on mountains.

BIRDS AND CARBON

The time arrives
when wiping traces of carbon off with their sleeves
poets return to the season of birds.

We recognize birds by their poses
the fleeting arcs of flight
the same arcs tour guides make with pointers
when stopping along the streets of
Waterloo, Ithaca, Cairo, Berlin . . . .

That's where history, mine and everyone's,
rests for a moment to take a deep breath.
Time stands still
the rest of life but smoke, luggage lifted and set down,
a conductor's small flag waving in our imaginations.

I can't remember the last time I held my breath—
was it summer? August? The sky scratched
with fresh red lines
like a gardener's palm. A pair of birds
joyfully encircled my home.
I exhaled, and a lone tree quivering in a field
transformed them into two pieces of paper
condemned to forever
somersault in the wind.

PENINSULA

My shadow stretches over the street
peninsula of fear
with coordinates that shake in the wind
like last week's wet blankets
hung out to dry.

The frightened child or the nervous woman
(the last brushstroke is missing)
the trembling border that separates them
the zigzag of smoke
from a forgotten cigarette.

At first I had only one eye
big and blue and dilated . . .
Now I have two
and a strip of sand between them
that dries and thickens
from day to day.

And a wind constantly shifting directions
pursuing clues left by the fossils
of extinct fish.

relentlessly pursues its daily ration
like a cat circling the cracked
            plate of my patience,
scrounging for what it can find.

It slinks between the feet
of those gathered around the table
the glare of a television screen
from across the room
floating like a glacier
through our frozen imaginations.

Mother's voice rustles, wrinkling the silence.
"Winter is nearing . . . we have to fix the door . . . "

Her daughter burns blue as an alcohol flame
and the molecules of air that surround her
reproduce, splitting and multiplying
impregnating themselves
drowning with desire for the distant seas.

THE WOMAN AND THE SCISSORS

I remember the scissors
that cut thick strips of newspaper
to seal cracks on stove pipes
and the scissors that trimmed my soft nails
delicate as pleurae

and later on
my sister's small scissors that cut
the silk thread of her embroidery, blue loops
wound tightly round two fingers of her right hand
while I watched a man shoveling snow
and heard rocks struck
and saw an acacia tree
branches covered in ice
swaying majestically, conspicuously,
like a nine-year-old on a swing,
with green bangs
and white stockings.

And then came my escape from the anxiety of scissors
an all-consuming appetite for books
the betrayal of my parents' simple dream:
a tailor's large scissors
tracing white chalk lines.

THE WOMAN AND THE GIRAFFES

The woman remembers:
once she was a member
of a family of giraffes
their skin so warm
it baked the air to terra cotta.
A giraffe's strength resides in its neck
in its long and muscled neck.
Its suffering, too, resides in the neck
in its bending over tropical trees.

One day, the entire herd was blotted out.
Their heads, slender knees, spotted backs, gone.
Only necks remained, oblique giraffe necks
confounded amidst blank paper
like boarding ladders on an airport runway
clumsily dragging themselves along
after the planes take off.

WINTER

Winter approaches
the bothersome sound of flies and cicadas dwindling.
Light fades over the poker game
the moon transplanted into the sky
like a healthy kidney into a weak body.
The pain lifts
but we remain lost, confused,
cloaked in condensation
like a busy downtown phone booth.

Venetian blinds slide shut
slicing off fingers of streetlight.
Tattered, dark squares alternate
where birds cross in migration,
a wall from which paintings are being removed.
An unconscious man's dream in black and white
is stopped short by a nurse's cough.
My body pressed against your ribs through the long night
like the earth by its latitudes, my last geographical memories
lying in frayed maps deep inside the city archives.

In the morning, mother stands in the same place
preparing coffee
plump, clean, healthy as an Easter egg.
Afraid of decalcification, the inevitable,
afraid of shattering.

CHAMOMILE BREATH

We never talk about death, mother
like married people who never speak of sex
doctors who never mention blood
the postman who no longer realizes he is holding his
       breath.

But fear of it graces everything you touch
the way a cotton field quivers
as a man strides through it.

In the morning
your chamomile breath
rises over the wrinkled pillow
adorned with white ubiquitous strands of hair
and black metal clips.

Don't wait for death to come noisily, mother,
dressed in wild, colored cloth
bells on its elbows and knees
like the Man of Carnivals
or a morris dancer at the end of May.

You will see instead a child with spindly legs
and a thick crop of hair
a child who never had the chance to grow up.
Haven't you ever heard the saying:
death is so close to birth
they are like nostrils on a face
on the verge of a sneeze.

AND THE SUN IS EXTINGUISHED

And the sun is extinguished
like the little red light that disappears
when the elevator stops.

I can't remember which is our floor—
the third, fifth, or the hundred and first . . .
but it always ends the same way:
a slap of cold air
the look of impatience
on the faces of those
waiting to get on.

PERHAPS MY MOTHER

She remembers her wedding
and the levy that followed—
three children with patched knees
little sharks
shadowing the white wreath of a ship.

She remembers the black violin
on the shelf
the depressions in its body
and on her husband's shirts
the impression of scaffolding,
concrete. She remembers
the petroleum pipeline, her harsh voice
dirty pockets, the hairs over her lip.
She remembers the neighbors' tiled rooftops sloping
into her small courtyard and the riverwind
scavenging, swallowing back days.

She remembers the cold, bruised
hands of midwives
inside her
fire irons poking coal
into flame.

She remembers the sick baby
her frantic fingers
on the morgue window
a dead soldier's
protruding feet.

I've never met this woman.
I only know the details
and a sweet old woman frightened out of superflous sleep.
Perhaps my mother
an apple tree and cypress grafted together
a flickering neon light.

NOCTURNE. SOFT WHISTLE

Now I imagine you, mother,
as you nap, snoring, one breast
sunk like a moon into sweet waters.
Are you frightened by thoughts of the insulin
the doctor prescribed this morning?
My little, old mother
past tense
or future past
wrapped inside the gray shawl
of an acrylic poem.

Sleep is short
there is hardly time
to dream about what life once held for you:
one white child, one black child
chasing a ball of yarn along the rug.

I know the way you startle awake.
I know the shattered door
at the entrance to your glass house.

But don't let me disturb your nap
with the swirling of my imagination,
a flock of zinc birds flying low to the ground.
Even in my dreams I cannot quell
the waves slapping against the hull
of a boat that follows the current.

THE NIGHT WILL SOON BE OVER . . .

When night arrives
trees strip off their shadows . . .

and
quarrel in the warm lake.

The moon's white calves
flash through the rushes.

The owl's eye
like a drop of mercury
slides across the nude body of the world.

A few more hours
and the night will be over . . .

remaining only in the pleats of a black cloak
slung over the branches of a cypress tree.

MORE THAN A RETROSPECTIVE

I was born of a dead hope
like a sprig of grass
between sidewalk slabs.

I learned my first words
behind an ill-fitted door.

I came to understand
the properties of light and darkness
through the cracks in my body
a clay body not wholly fired.

I learned to sing
the way a cold draft learns to navigate
between two clumsy lovers.

But like a whore's dirty underpants
I am not growing used to sadness . . .

One dead hope
catches up to the next
like one bus approaching another
then the stop.

CLEAR HOURS

During clear hours
I am like the lonely hunchbacked tree
        on the slope of a hill.
Beneath my shade
rest weary travelers.

I count the rings around my trunk
I count the knots and navels
I scratch beneath my cracked bark—
a woman's nightmare.

I count white days, warm days
I count the rotations of the sun rolling
into darkness, I count nights of moonlight
nights of lightning
when I embrace you from behind, when I pull away from you
as streams of water from a shower tile.

I count yellow days
and tighten my grip on the test tube of all days.
Many are the friends who disappear
few who return.
        My black blood circulates, my black memory
turns back on itself
and drowns
in the primeval silence of creation.

SUNDAY BELLS

My soul
beats like a tongue
against the side of a bell.

Listen.
It's the Sunday bells
the Sunday bells of high mass
when the priest preaches forgiveness
and we all lay flowers on graves.

WHAT IS KNOWN

The search for unknown words
is a complete failure.
They have all been discovered.
They are round and soft, without mystery
little planets festering with ants too tired
to mount a hobo's shoe.

Rosary in hand
the words count crimson drops
of silence dripping from above
and repeat themselves over and over
like demented men.

But they take pride in their age.
After all, they are exhibits in a museum
and I, transitory, passing before them
can only cloud their glass
with my breath.

II

FRESCO

Now there is no gravity. Freedom is meaningless.
I weigh no more than a hair
on a starched collar.
Lips meet in the ellipsis at the end of a drowning
confession; on the sand, a crab closes its claws hermetically
and moves one step forward and two steps to the right.
It was long ago when I first broke into a shudder
at the touch of your fingers;
no more shyness, no more healing, no more death.
Now I am light as an Indian feather, and can easily reach
            the moon
a moon clean as an angel's sex
on the frescoes of the church.
Sometimes I can even see asteroids dying like drones
in ecstasy for their love, their queen.

ELECTROLYTES

For a long time now
your kisses have burned me
and your clean body frightened me
like sheets in a surgery ward
and your breath disappearing in my lungs
is like lilies dropped into a cesspool
in the dead of winter.

For a long time now
I have felt ashamed of my freedom.
Every day I pull a stake off your fence
and burn it for warmth.

My freedom . . . your freedom . . .
An atmosphere alive with electricity
my soul pawned for a nickel
yours slowly deserted by its ions
and growing smaller every day.

ALWAYS A PREMONITION

A premonition? The reek of alcohol
on the postman's breath
when he delivered yesterday's mail?

A premonition
always arriving before me
like an ostrich testing out its legs.

Every step it takes
marks my tardiness.
There's always a sign, a thick, greasy feather
plucked from a regal plume.

By accident
you wipe away my kisses
along with your shaving cream, there, by your ears.
A premonition . . . another premonition.
I ought to be more careful. Ants grow restless
when the dampness sets in. Always a premonition . . .
I'm tired of the daily routines,
a vacuum cleaner wiping away dust
breathing in tomorrow's unpredictability
black wire wound round my leg.

TEST

Tested at every turn
like a noun
in declension.

In the existential ablative
nails sprout from my imagination
like case endings aligned
by my dead cells.

In the genitive
I chase the dwarf
who stripped off my chain
of lymphocytes
dried out by the moon.
And in the dative I'm quiet
bending over myself
crushing parasites at night
in the encampments.

Whereas in the nominative and accusative
I am Narcissus, naked.
Someday, alone,
I'll drown in my own
dreams.

SO LONG AS

So long as we still reflect each other—
even deformed—as through silver spoons,
wine glasses, and exultant bottles
on the table of a dinner party about to begin,
things can't be that bad.
But, eventually, steam
rolls in through the kitchen door
like a ghost without a soul
and then . . .
and then . . .

WITH A PIERCING CLARITY

You complain that your shoulders grow cold
that you cannot stay naked till midnight.
Lust clings to the dark sides of our bodies.

The yellow lampshade clicks off
and darkness swallows light
like a starfish consuming black prey
in its muscular belly.
I hear only the rhythmic breathing
of a smoldering fire
licking its pink bones.
The dried-up leaf of timidity crumbles
circles rotate over our faces like crossed eyes . . .
Fear in its postmodern form
is similar to what we had once known—
the clarity of the window
we stood in front of
before the hungry images shattered.

OVER THE ICY MAGMA OF YOUR GRAY CURIOSITY

Over the icy magma of your gray curiosity
I stride barefooted so I can feel every change
and it hurts.
I feel a wilted palm sprout between my shoulder blades
like uncertain lightning between sheepfolds.
I feel a cold eye, a shrew's burrow under water,
a fear that remains a chain of mute consonants.
It blows across us yet there is no wind.
We are like sails lowered in good weather.

A heart nailed to a door is a red lantern
illuminating only those who leave.
What emanates from inside is our demise—
grass spreading over the rib cage
of an old metal-frame chest.

FROST

Predictably, the first frost arrived
simplifying what we saw.
The atmosphere began to hibernate
into the realm of hypothesis.

First you touched the inviting flora of my eyes
then the untrodden earth
with its subtle memory of grain
(my fingers now held tight).
Then, after the clay, you touched upon
our ancient apprehensions, irresponsibility,
vengeance for a story left untold.

And on and on until you reached a layer of water.
Can you hear it flowing?
This is my vivid core, you can't go any deeper.
And yet you do . . . further and further. We were wrong.
Here the elemental world of cold metals begins—
here identity, weight, gravitational forces end,
where I can no longer be I.

Frost arrived, the scene sufficiently simplified
the sound of an accordion, roads cordoned off,
breath freezing at the first syllable
turning to beautiful coral
transforming into coral.

THE BED

My bed, a temple
where murmurs of a stifled prayer press
against my palate.

Frozen genitalia
buried fruit, imperfect fruit
clean green leaves stretching out beneath the blankets

to reach you, your warmth
dew on the skin of a morning dream.
A mole like a coffee bean on your back
arms that rarely hold me
and my eyes, rocks of salt
brought ashore by the tide.

My bed is not a bed, but a temple:
we change sheets as often
as the religious replace candles.
We leave our shoes in a neat row outside the door.
The heads of sacrificed birds roll up the stairs
to where we are throbbing, a single being split in half
martyred by silence.

ABSENCE

The moon
nicotine of a kiss . . .

A sideways glance
like the mast of a pirate ship
beyond a distant island.

SILENCE

You and I
and two empty coffee cups

and some fugitive word
struggling in a spider's web
to save its life.

Twenty nails
lie on the table
like shells spilled
from a child's torn pocket
onto asphalt.

Outside
the morning air
chews its leftovers.

Our eyes remain
fixed on the empty cups
shapes of distant cosmos
drowning in sediment . . .

A shadow stretches its body
along the wall
and douses the candle's flame

a flame lighting two thin wrists
poorly bandaged wrists.

OUR WORDS HAVE GROWN OLD

Our clothes have worn out
our shoes leak
speech grows old . . .

We look into each other's eyes
swallow cold food
and once in a while a word
trembles in the air
like the feathers of a bird
with its head chopped off.

FRAIL BONES

Why are you calling me?
What can I do for you now?
What can I do for the voice shaking like a cut wire
saying, "I am exiled,
and have nothing left but a pen-and-paper coffin . . . "

Dismal thoughts cross my mind—
hunchbacked, presumptuous, slammed
like empty kettles against
the army's kitchen wall.

What do you want from me at this hour?
The water around you has receded
and you are ugly as a desert gorge,
as the moon's potbelly hanging over a glacier.

This is what happens
when you give nothing of yourself
when you kiss a pregnant woman
you never intend to marry.
Your eyes are red
as putrid meat
from your withered shoulderblades
hangs a rattlesnake
(umbilical cord that
feeds you nothing but air).

I am evicted;
like the stone of the Chinese Oracle
my feeble soul
cannot fit into its cube-shaped house.

TRUTH

Truth is always someone else's privilege.
Lock your doors until it passes over you
as the Jews did in Egypt.
If it reaches your mouth, don't be merciful.
Chew it up like a piece of liver
and force it to withdraw into your own bitterness.
If you try to spit it out
I'll be there to scold you
my curses isolating you more each day
your broad bare shoulders forlorn as basilicas.

So recently banished, we keep stopping to ask
why we are here, why we were born
covered with a single leaf
molded by a potter's filthy palm.

Were we always looking for a clean body to lean on—
Could this be a story of thistles
left to soak in the sunlight?
Let me touch you. There is only one real truth:
that which the hand feels.
The rest is white mist
rising from a Turkish bath
hovering into eternity.

Truth is someone else's privilege.
Don't you know that by now?
We could never have borne
the loneliness of water
could never have balanced
like two stone angels on the lip of a fountain.

THE BLOSSOMING ALMOND BRANCH

You never know when love will reappear
like an eagle above the sea
tracing us with a deep penetrating gaze.

It may come when old age has knocked us down
and the smallest shock will undo us.
It will be painful to face in the morning
when with all its grandeur sunlight
unfolds upon a blossoming almond branch
arched over a crumbling wall.

And the sun will never reach its zenith.
Like a pumpkin it grows horizontally
dreaming under the green leaves of a garden.

It's exactly here where we first met.
You were a sealed white envelope.
If I came any closer to you
wax would stick to my chest
and the message would be lost forever.

Look at that hand with its slim and delicate fingers
spread on the wall, that morning ray.
It's not a challenge to us. It reaches out in generosity.

And the roads that will lead you to Alaska
awaken. The wooden signs left behind at barred mines
struggle to recall the damaged syllables, to remember
coal cars emerging from the warm underworld.

STILL LIFE

Here in a summer full of dust
the dampness of winter
trails us into dark corners.

I bought the shoes days ago
but they remain untouched in the box
heel to heel.

Blessed is the sunbeam that falls upon us
like the eye of a stranger focused on a *natura morte*.
A platter of the season's finest fruit
so plump, and nestled among it, a shiny dagger.
It's not dangerous
but as alluring and peaceful
as the fruit that surrounds it.

What has become of us?
My hands, skillful and transparent,
slice the atmosphere into rabbit feed.

Another new pair of shoes
to help you enjoy a stroll around the grounds.
Since you've left I dream of only one thing:
the sound they would make
in the evening
as you reach the front door.

THE HABITUAL

The wind slashes its own face.

The cold metallic glare
of a broken needle
in the rough coat of speech.

On a thunderbolt's edge
teeth are sharpened . . .

At night my dreams quake
the bed with their incestuous love-making.
They have the same blood type
but won't recognize each other in the morning.

Tracks along a wet floor . . .
I'll wake when the sad dog's paw
scratches the door
at midnight.

WITHIN ANOTHER IDIOM

I could have been born in another place
within another idiom
and stood beside another
in perfect harmony, or in utter chaos.
If only I could be reborn
and drift between bald dolls and my parents' hands—
different parts of the selfsame boat.
A woman's steely voice hovers above me
but I am a chestnut wrapped in green thistle
ripening under the feet of exhausted pedestrians.

I ought to wear my old sweater again
the one the color of a hepatitis-stricken sun
and reread love letters from schoolboys
their round, fleshy syllables mushrooming off the page.
I ought to listen more closely to the sound the wind makes
scampering against a narrow pane of glass.

And, all the while, the scent of rosemary, rosemary
the consolatory rosettes blossoming on walls . . .

Like a Moslem cloak—a cloak wound round me
several times, round my bosom, oh my bosom
pitch-black valleys—the innocence
        of the world could suffocate me.

But, at last . . .
I can only hope for any laceration

any tear in the nylon net which gathers us together
and drags us along
until the moment our bodies, covered in scales
feel the dry burn of salt.

BETRAYED

Betrayed woman, like an outgrown shirt
like the worn hole on an old belt
like a starched collar . . .
Betrayed woman, who wakes from nightmares
feeling like dirt in the corner of an eye
like a kettle taken off the stove
still steaming.

Her hips sway rhythmically
in a chewing motion
as she moves diagonally through the house.
The children, oh the children, bubbling forth!
Late at night, an aluminum lid
above a sprig of parsley—
limp nerve floating in a cold lemony broth.

There is a betrayed man, too,
betrayed by dark angels
with shoulders covered in ferns.

Betrayed men and women
accept fate nobly
as one would accept a murky glass of water
at a rest stop along the way.
Betrayed men and women
on a long journey.

III

ONCE AGAIN ABOUT MY FATHER

Forgive me, father, for writing this poem
that sounds like the creak of a door
against a pile of rags
in a room with cobwebs in its armpits
a cold so bitter it stops your blood.

The same old black-and-white television
deformed images in its chest
the same old threadbare bedspread
like the face of a menopausal woman.
Next to a lamp, Adam's shriveled apple,
a hunger in your washed-out eyes.

You remember to ask me about something
when a toothpick snaps between your teeth.

I know how it is with you now, father:
by now you are content with loneliness—
its corpse in minus four degrees centigrade
its aluminum siding
its brace of dust
its calm sterility, infinitely white.

THE MOON IN NOVEMBER

The moon in November.
Lightning sucks
the warm blood of summer.

A bell
tolled by the deaf-mute.

The winds make love
in rusted cans.

A memory—
the scarecrow's sleeve
draped
over cut stalks.

The moon
an antique brass coin
that can only be traded
for a drunkard's iris.

The moon in November
a throat rising and lowering
to the tune of rumination.

Alas, here is the small airport covered in frost
and here the plane that takes off
leaving it behind the way a chipped tooth abandons a boxer.

That town remains behind forever
with its new and dry bridges
resembling women gone astray
its many churches a flock of eagles
watching out over a singular abyss.
The house with two gates
covered in late August rain
my euphoric steps upon its wooden floor
synchronized with the hammering
of a man who abhors the concept of time.
He taught me to hold fast to my skin
as the darkness holds up walls
in a building under construction.

The plane emerges from a large barren cloud
and old men slumber in it
like half-whitewashed trees.

Further along, the plane flutters amid mysterious air pockets
and my body crackles like a handful of twigs in winter.
It's the fox that holds fast to its old den
it's the spirit that returns at dawn. Here everything begins . . .

YEARLY SNOW

In this city the yearly snow
leaning on sparse, lonesome trees
doesn't mean a thing.
It signifies nothing more
than the meandering of a veteran
leaning on a wooden crutch.

The same war story told a hundred times
the same brand of cigarette distributed by friendly hands
and those same eyes hovering, dark and lazy.
Only that. And the dry rhythmic knocking
until his silhouette disappears
amidst the shadows cast down by rooftops
their melting snow dripping
in terrible slowness . . .

CHRONIC APPENDICITIS

How odd this winter is.
A felled tree in a forest
hallucinates skeletons
dragged out of the body.

Wet kisses on a bed of wet leaves
the shudder of a notary's hand
curving symmetrically against a sky
covered in paper and glue.

The inner light of things would be enough
to fuel our chlorophyll
for we are as free as germs . . .
we are frail trees, gracious plants,
half our bodies
bent in the wind.

The exhalation of cars in traffic
the exhalation of a dying February:
carbon dioxide creaking forth from lungs
like bedsprings in an orphanage.

February's edict slowly expires
and again rain, rain, and more rain—
rain moaning under the excruciating suffering
of chronic appendicitis
rain without thunder, without lightning.

HALF PAST THREE

Half past three. The hour when all matter
separates into cause and effect.
My bed floats in the shallow waters of a lagoon
its legs cast in bronze
gripping the carpet.

An ax strikes rhythmically
against the sequoia trunk
of world harmony.
The same old history
no winners or losers . . .

The beginning and the end, both cryptic and vague:
two midwives pushing cruelly at my belly. Nearby,
like a burnt-out log
a cat, bored of being stroked,
dozes on its paws.

Half past three in the morning, my elements break down
into air, water, fire, earth,
until I am unrecognizable.

I am not my own enemy. My enemy is the light.
And the Yellow River of China.
With the tragic history
of bridges arching over it.

ON A NIGHT LIKE THIS

On a night like this lightning
bounds unexpectedly across fields of corn.
Thunder, ghost of a stampeding herd,
flashes black and white on celluloid
the stench of dirt and flesh
ready to escape
its own silhouette.

Restless as two mountain ranges
we dream the same dreams:
small, white clouds pissing
like little boys behind the school wall.

THE AWAKENING OF THE EREMITE

All ideas escape me
one by one, secretly slipping away
like witnesses to a political crime.

When they crawl back, tortoise-slow
the air trembles nervously in its wheelchair
and I rise.

My shadow, liberated, wanders
the room on an invisible cord
gravity sudden as a dead fly
dropped from a spider's nest.

All ideas escape me—
how far this time I cannot say.
Perhaps they'll turn up in a train station somewhere
in a town where they are unwelcome.

Outside, the moon presses against the hills
like a prophet's tongue against his palate.

The walls, protesting,
return my voice two, three, four times over
an echo horribly replicating itself
while slowly inside me
the eremite awakens.

THE ALMSHOUSE

In the yard, between the stones
grass withers
beneath the weight of a walking stick.

Inside, dentures float
in glasses of water
like bottled messages
that will never be read
drifting in a rising sea.

ANTIPASTORAL

If only there could be three more snowfalls
before clouds descend upon the green mountains
and the forest's suffering reemerges from beneath tree bark.

From radios the name "Aisha" echoes meaninglessly,
an oval foreboding turning like an oriental bracelet around
          a dark ankle.
Local inhabitants speak of the now legendary Red Fox.

The fires doze . . . hunters clean their guns.
Tomorrow will be a fine day for a chase.
At dusk they'll return with torches that shudder like quails,
shaking the moon's white cubes off their boots.

Meanwhile worms burrowing into wood
make a ceaseless grating sound
oblivious to the hasty prayers of those seated around the table.
And the wind howls in vain, to no end,
like a senile dog on the kitchen floor, licking its calves
while eyeing a string of red jalapeño peppers.

OUT OF BOREDOM

Out of boredom
roebucks lie down with toads
night swallows the moon
like a sleeping pill
and sky becomes lace
on the veil of a dreamer.
A white strand of smoke rises
like a cypress
from a burning cigarette.

The clock tower warbles a soldier's old tune
the one he whistles as he polishes his steel crutches.
An old woman's fingers, anxious as a child's
held out for a nickel, tap a tarot card.

Out of boredom
footsteps consume the streets
with the hunger of Chaplin in a silent film.
Out of boredom the soul, like an amoeba,
expands and divides
so that it will no longer be alone.

HEATHEN REJOICING

Your lips
rugged as a cliff
a cliff hunched over the geometric plane
of my conscience
drawn taut to breaking.

From the depths of the Bible
our clay statues awaken
to complete the cycle of love and loneliness.
Your mouth on the screen
a black hole—
anti-time.

We worship our graven images
clay statues
earthen idols
so that we can turn the clocks back
to times of innocence
the heathen rejoicing.

QUITE BY ACCIDENT

Regardless
I recognized your face
struck by the car's green grill.
I felt
and smelled
in the desert wind
your face, your hand
along my spine.
A clock spring broke
and I wailed
like a bucket hitting the bottom
of a dried-up well.

But now I know we are strangers
and happen to have passed one another quite by accident
like two photographs
on the front page of the daily newspaper.

SELF-DEFENSE

Confined
to a tent of soldiers
who will never return home.
If you try to leave
you will step on the bodies
sleeping beside you.

You have nowhere to go.
The stars
those witches' fingernails
stir your destiny through the fog.

In the corner
among ashes
you count the holes in your old blanket.
You breathe in bits of everyone's dreams.
Like an iceberg you ignore all borders.

While in your blood
surprisingly enough
the leukocytes multiply.

NO TIME

You asked for death, you were tired.
You asked for it so easily
as if calling for the white horse
with a bag of oats.
You did not know your destiny lay
in a bullet, dripping with blood,
extracted from your body.

It was December 1950.
The murder notice
blackened newspapers like a rotted tooth.
The river froze to a razor's edge
olive trees nearly snapped
beneath the weight of their dark fruit.

Death came silently, without a grave.
We were even afraid of your body.
On my palms were bloody scratches, thorny roses.
I did not know where to hide them.

You died during the revolution.
There was no time to bury you.
You left simply, as quietly as those moments when
wearing a decrepit soldier's coat
we wait on a platform for the next train.

IN THE HOME OF THE DEAD MAN

In the home of the dead man
the lights stay on till midnight
like toppled sand dunes
beneath a red sky
a flock of blackbirds.
A felt hat left behind
by the last visitor
coffee rank
as the darkened armpits
of men wearing white shirts.
With the greatest ease this afternoon
we launched a boat into black waters
and cried: "Swim!"

In the home of the dead man
a bed is missing.
So is a wooden stake from the yard—
details nobody has noticed.
Gone too are the stars
the shepherd once with his crook
drove across the sky
to keep them away
from gardens and houses.

NIGHT LANDSCAPE

An anaconda of suspicion
twists through
this endless night.

A moonbeam treads
blindly over the bed
like King Edyp's* hand.
My fingers touch
the sleeping baby's hair.
Oh, Lord, how coarse
the roots churned up
by my body's erosion.

Like tattoos on a pirate's arm
anguish is drawn terribly
on faces.

Perhaps later I will sleep
and night's ebb
will embrace me in its salty profundity
like a lost shoe
washed ashore.

*Oedipus, in Albanian.

FAREWELL, SUNNY DAYS

He who checked out yesterday
had the look of an amnesiac
and a little sand in the small lock of his suitcase.

Tomorrow it's my turn
to return the key, still warm, to the reception desk
my skin stripped down, yet somehow thicker.
I'll leave behind the remnants of a tired soul
the way one might leave change for the waiter
dressed in white shirt and black bow tie.

Farewell warm days, sunny days
in white shirt
and black bow tie.

WATCHING THEM NAP

When I lay you down my darlings
in the foggy drowsiness of a hot afternoon
dozing lightly
you are two white Mediterranean villages
under a gray sky.

The breath of my little girl
the twinkling of a barley field
mingles with my nicotine breath—
strands of blond hair
on the weathered shoes of a barber.

Saturday evening is smooth
as a porcelain bath
from whose water a knee emerges
and sometimes a white elbow—
stars that survived the night.

My shadow drifts through the rooms
with my eternal anguish
watching you, my loves,
as I would watch anything innocent in this world.

And when one day you come to understand this
your pasts will converge into a single instant
all calm ending with a short cutting whistle
like the last drops of water
whirling down the tub's metal drain.

A MUTUAL UNDERSTANDING
for Lea

I can't escape your sunflower-gaze.
Do not judge me for what I lack—
a mother's instinct
which like a water bottle grown cold
ends up at the foot of the bed.

Understand me: we are alike, you and I,
yielding to the everlasting intricacies
between two people.
Like you
I too think of our lives as a thing without history
an apple you bite once
then throw away without remorse.

HALF-CUBISM

Mosquitoes stick to the wet paint
on the portrait in which I am still
twenty years old.
Dusk rubs up against
the run-down factory railing
like a heifer scratching its back.

And nowhere else can people
be found taking such pride
in their descendance from clay
as here at the seaside.
The moon relieves its bladder
in the last romantic corner
between concrete block buildings
packed tight with anxiety.

Across the road a disco
swells with lights
rumbles like a gorilla pounding its chest
trying impossibly to say "I love you . . . "
And the yellow grass whispers with relief
as a blond boy returns from a casual fuck
alone through the darkening field.

SEASONS CHANGE

As seasons change
windows darken
coffee stains the corners of lips.
The old rusty stars
wipe clean off the body.

As seasons change
the trees wail
their shadows swelling over the river

the worms rehabilitated
the flies and birds repatriated
maggots and snakes deported to their homeland

and along the border we wait pale-faced
fake passports in our hands.

The green breath of sheep at the slaughteryard
the purple breath of bells unpondered
invades the air.
Ghosts emerge bleached white
from dark corridors
like stilts in the rain.

We line up at bus stations
the schedules unchanged
the cloud formation incestuous and ashamed
constricting above the barren hills.

Seasons change
rhythmically and without fail
like guards at the great institution
crossing through the trapezoidal shadow
cruel and gray.

Afterword

In May 1996, I had the good fortune to visit Albania at a unique crossroads in its history: the five-year interlude between the fall of the Communist regime and the collapse of the governing Democratic Party. The atmosphere in Tirana was festive and full of energy. Along the main avenue in its city center new bars and cafés, where young men and women smoked and flirted, had cropped up every few yards. There were more Mercedes-Benzes on the roads than I could count. The scene might have been lifted from a quaint Italian town but for the backdrop of Stalinist-era buildings on which were painted, in the emblematic style of Socialist Realism, workers uprising against their oppressors. That, and an elderly man dragging a lamb, still very much alive, by its hind legs, its head bobbing against the pavement.

I came to Albania to meet a few poets whose voice had enthralled me, Luljeta Lleshanaku among them. Lleshanaku was the youngest by perhaps a decade, but in many ways her work felt to me the most experienced. The lines of her verse that fell so softly, naturally onto the page carried an immense sadness. At the same time, I was drawn to the intense yearning in her images, not a longing for an idealistic past, but for a future that could never be, as it would forever be burdened by a troublesome history. I felt myself moving through her haunting landscapes, helpless, trapped. The melancholy of these finely etched worlds seemed diametrically opposed to the new wave of optimism in downtown Tirana, yet I couldn't help feeling that the reality of Lleshanaku's poems lurked just under the city's surface.

Lleshanaku is an engaging woman with an overworked, weary, look. One sees in her, as in many Balkan people, history's raw, crushing impression. Her gaze—hungry, determined, unrelenting—is that of a survivor, someone who has overcome great adversity. We meet in her office, a large cavernous space in the institutional-looking Dajti Hotel that houses the newspaper *Zeri i rinise*, for which she serves as editor in chief. The only light in the room is from sunlight that seeps like fog through a dusty window, but in Lleshanaku's eyes burns a birdlike energy. Not long after meeting her one realizes she has a tendency to confront people with difficult, personal questions. Passionate about important subjects, she is intolerant and saddened by the inanity of small talk. What she hungers for is true contact, compassion, conversation.

She is quiet but tough, and her raw brand of honesty and biting humor can offend as quickly as her innocence and sincerity draw one back in. She can be as direct, critical, and perversely funny as she is in her poems, where, for instance, she states that "your breath disappearing in my lungs / is like lilies dropped into a cesspool."

In her verse, joy lives side by side with melancholy in a kind of symbiotic contradiction. Her lines can be exalting, playful, often bursting with a sense of wonder that is unmistakably youthful, and almost naïve. Her poems are highly imagistic, the connections between images precociously and precariously intuitive. They are, for the most part, short, contained studies, still lifes rendered abstractly, yet they soar within the boundless imagination of a speaker who delights in the sensual, the tactile, who "light as an Indian feather … can easily reach the moon" and witnesses "asteroids dying like drones / in ecstasy for their love, their queen."

Her apartment building is typical for Tirana, the ground outside strewn with rubble and broken cinder blocks amongst which children and stray cats play. Inside, her apartment is small and modestly furnished. As in my neighborhood in New York, every space is lived in. But unlike my apartment, Lleshanaku's is not cluttered with papers, books, children's toys and laptop computers. Space, as in her poems, is a commodity not to be wasted.

While we speak her mother serves drinks and snacks. At

one point, her six-year-old daughter runs in excitedly from play-
ing out on the street, asking a question of Lleshanaku. The reply
is given tersely, with a stern love in her voice, and the girl, sat-
isfied, runs out again. I am comfortable here, and it's easy to for-
get where I am. But this is not just anywhere; this is Albania, a
county where nearly every family has to some degree, at one
time or another, fallen victim to oppression. Lleshanaku's fami-
ly is no exception. In fact, the extent to which her family has
been persecuted is sobering. Her maternal grandfather's brother
fought in a pro-Allied faction against the Italian, and then
German, occupiers in World War II. Directly following the war,
he found himself caught in another struggle—this time on the
losing side—against the Communist forces. After the Stalinists
came to power, as punishment, the entire family was sentenced
to five years in a prison camp. When one of Lleshanaku's uncles
attempted to escape, the family was tortured. Her mother was five
years old when they subjected her to electric shock. Her uncle
was arrested several more times and spent a total of twenty-seven
years in prison or internment camps.

Lleshanaku's paternal grandfather, too, played an instru-
mental role in the anti-Communist resistance after the war,
organizing armed insurgencies around the country. Following his
arrest, his family was also interred for many years, and he would
eventually die in prison. Her mother and father obviously had
much in common when they met and married in the small city
of Elbasan, both families being notoriously anathema to the
regime. Condemned to manual labor, her father worked as a
bricklayer and her mother made woolen filters for tractors.
Luljeta, born in 1968, remembers her mother arriving home
each night with wounds on her hands, which she spent the
evening treating so she could return to work the next morning.
Together Lleshanaku's parents carried the stigma of their family's
"shame"—which Luljeta and her sister would inherit from birth.

No family member of Lleshanaku's was allowed to pursue a
higher education, serve in public office, or even hold employ-
ment of any stature. They were treated as pariahs, denied any

form of approval whatsoever, down to the most ludicrous detail. When a television crew arrived to film her kindergarten class singing, five-year-old Luljeta was forbidden to take part. Throughout her schooling, no matter how impressive her academic performance, her name could not appear on the honor roll. When she questioned her teachers, she was told flat out that no accolades could be accorded her because her family was not in conformity with the Communist Party. Forbidden to enter college upon graduating high school, Lleshanaku went on to hold the only kind of job the state permitted her: she worked in a carpet factory. Walking home she would pass posters and signs that were aimed directly at people like her and her family: "Down with enemies of the working class," or "Let us remain steadfast against our *inner* and foreign enemies!"

In the fall of 1989, she married Lazer Stani—a prominent journalist for *Zeri i rinise* (ironically, the same newspaper that Lleshanaku would later head)—in a small private ceremony. A few months later, her passport was seized by the State Security and she was forbidden to leave the country, ostensibly because, according to the authorities, her cousins living in New York were collaborating against the regime. When authorities learned of her marriage, the editors of *Zeri i rinise* were given a political directive. Stani had the option of leaving his job or leaving his wife. Following his dismissal, they moved to Kllojka, a small town north of Tirana, where he was assigned a job as schoolteacher. At the same time, as petitions were being put together to return him to his job on the paper, government apparatchiks spread a rumor that Lazer and Luljeta had been killed crossing the border to Yugoslavia. But things were about to improve for the couple. The next two years would bring vast changes to Albania. In December 1990, the Communist Party accepted the presence of opposition parties, and in March 1992 free elections were held. The Democratic Party won in a landslide, promising a clean break with the past, complete freedom for its citizens, and grand investment opportunities for all.

When I met Lleshanaku in 1996, she was belatedly pursuing

the college education that had earlier been denied her. In only four years she had published three noteworthy books of poetry, including *Ysmëkubizëm* (*Half-Cubism*), which had received much praise that year. In 1992, the poet Dritëro Agolli, who had written the introduction to her first book, *Sytë e Somnambulës* (*The Sleepwalkers' Eyes*), confirmed what she had always suspected—before the fall of the regime, all publishers were forbidden to publish her poetry. Of all people he should know: for twenty years he served as the head of the Albanian Writers Union, the notorious arm of government censorship.

During my visit, Lleshanaku seemed to be in awe of the West, holding on to an idealized vision of the American dream that many Americans themselves had grown weary of decades before. And yet, while visiting New York a few years later, she never once wore her glasses. As I pointed out the Empire State Building and other landmarks, she didn't even bother looking up. "Freedom is meaningless," she writes in the title poem, "Fresco," by which she means both the word and its symbols. After all, Albanians had long grown used to empty symbolism, to a society that claimed ideological superiority while simultaneously imprisoning nearly a third of its population and suppressing the basic freedoms of the rest. Real freedom, for Lleshanaku, is something bred in the imagination, something generated from the inside, not forced inward. "In the existential ablative," she writes in the witty poem, "Test," "nails sprout from my imagination / like case endings aligned / by my dead cells." Western freedom is indicated by our ability to speak freely, openly, without fear or hesitation. To dream, to exchange ideas, to observe the human condition, the peculiarities of human relationships, to express them in verse, to have others read it. . . everyday choices, unnoticed by us, crucial to her.

Thirteen months after my visit, the ruling Democratic Party would be torn down in shame over an investment scandal, and the Socialist Party—including some former Communists still in prison awaiting trial for their crimes—would again be in control of the government. At the time, this was quite a blow to

Lleshanaku and others who had hoped to put the Communist era behind them. Thankfully, the newly constructed Socialist Party has so far been careful about turning back the clock on personal rights, and Albania remains a free and democratic country. "But what about Albania's future?" I recently asked Lleshanaku via e-mail. "Like a dormant volcano," she answered, "throughout history the Albanian people periodically erupt—not in order to cause damage, but to prove to the world that they are still alive." And the future of Albanian poetry? "Albanians have no shortage of things to write about," explained Lleshanaku, "and they need never look far to find a rich cultural heritage. But first," she said, "they must search inward—not to larger cultures or overarching ideologies—to find their inner rivers."

Luljeta Lleshanaku is young, and her poetry will surely continue to evolve. Like Albania, her work reinvents itself as outside influences continue to seep in. Her fourth collection, for example, is full of images of a New Hampshire winter where she spent two months. And yet this landscape is strangely *Albanized*—an isolated and lonely space that merges into the speaker's own body, a place where "identity, weight, gravitational forces end, / where I can no longer be I." The Albanian novelist Ridvan Dibra notes that her work is itself an attempt to open new worlds within its readers.

> When you close her book, the images don't leave you.
> They cleave you open like a leopard's paw, and enter
> into you. Once inside they create their own life, a second life, vastly different from the original. What more
> can we expect from real poetry, from true art?

Included in this collection are poems from all four of her books, but the bulk is assembled from the mature work of her third and fourth collections. A few new poems are included here as well. They are not arranged chronologically or even thematically. Rather, the order is constructed intuitively, using the poem "Memory," a philosophical rumination on memory real and memory historic, as a point of departure. Although this is a book of selected poetry, it may be better referred to as a book of selected early poems. At thirty-four years old, Lleshanaku is extraordinarily accomplished, but there is no predicting the heights her work will climb to in years to come.

HENRY ISRAELI

Bibliography

POEMS LISTED BY BOOKS

The Sleepwalker's Eyes (*Sytë e Somnambulës*, Artemida, 1992): "And the Sun Us Extinguished"; "Our Words Have Grown Old."

Sunday Bells (*Këmbanat e Së Dielës*, Shtëpia Botuese e Lidhjes së Shkrimatarëve, 1994): "Perhaps My Mother"; "The Night Will Soon Be Over…"; "Sunday Bells"; "Absence"; "Silence"; "The Habitual"; "The Moon in November"; "The Almshouse"; "Self-Defense"; "Night Landscape."

Half-Cubism (*Ysmëkubizëm*, Eurorilindja, 1996): "Peninsula"; "Neurosis"; "Winter"; "Nocturne. Soft Whistle"; "More Than a Retrospective"; "What Is Known"; "Fresco"; "Electrolytes"; "Test"; "So Long As"; "The Bed"; "Frail Bones"; "Once Again About My Father"; "Yearly Snow"; "Chronic Appendicitis"; "The Awakening of the Eremite"; "Out of Boredom"; "Quite by Accident"; "No Time"; "Farewell, Sunny Days"; "Half-Cubism"; "Seasons Change."

Antipastoral (*Antipastorale*, Eurorilindja, 1999): "Memory"; "The Woman and the Scissors"; "The Woman and the Giraffes"; "Chamomile Breath"; "Clear Hours"; "Always a Premonition"; "With a Piercing Clarity"; "Over the icy magma of your gray curiosity"; "Frost"; "Truth"; "Within Another Idiom"; "Betrayed"; "Only the Beginning"; "Half Past Three"; "On a Night Like This"; "Antipastoral"; "Heathen Rejoicing"; "In the Home of the Dead Man"; "Watching Them Nap"; "A Mutual Understanding."

New Poems: "Birds and Carbon"; "The Blossoming Almond Branch"; "Still Life."

POEMS LISTED BY TRANSLATOR

Ukzenel Buçpapa: "The Night Will Soon Be Over"; ""More Than a Retrospective"; "What Is Known"; "Fresco"; "Electrolytes"; "Absence"; "Silence"; "Our Words Have Grown Old"; "The Habitual"; "The Moon in November"; "The Awakening of the Eremite"; "The Almshouse"; "Quite by Accident"; "Self-Defense"; "Seasons Change."

Noci Deda: "Winter."

Alban Kupi: "Sunday Bells"; "So Long As"; "No Time"; "Farewell, Sunny Days."

Albana Lleshanaku: "Memory"; "Peninsula"; "Neurosis"; "The Woman and the Scissors"; "Chamomile Breath"; "The Bed"; "Once Again About My Father"; "Yearly Snow": "Watching Them Nap"; "Half-Cubism."

Luljeta Lleshanaku: ""Perhaps My Mother"; "Nocturne. Soft Whistle"; "Still Life."

Lluka Qafoku: "The Woman and the Giraffes"; "And the Sun Is Extinguished."

Shpresa Qatipi: "Birds and Carbon"; "Always a Premonition"; "Test"; "With a Piercing Clarity"; "Over the icy magma of your gray curiosity"; "Frost"; "Truth"; "The Blossoming Almond Branch"; "Within Another Idiom"; "Betrayed"; "Only the Beginning"; "On a Night Like This"; "Antipastoral"; "Heathen Rejoicing"; "In the Home of the Dead Man"; "Night Landscape"; "A Mutual Understanding."

Qazim Sheme: "Clear Hours"; "Frail Bones"; "Chronic Appendicitis"; "Out of Boredom."

Daniel Weissbort: "Half Past Three."

All poems cotranslated by Henry Israeli, with the following exceptions: Joanna Goodman cotranslated "Self-Defense," "Perhaps My Mother," and "Test."

Index of Titles and First Lines